T0306978

# Ten Principles for Building Healthy Places

**Thomas W. Eitler**

**Edward T. McMahon**

**Theodore C. Thoerig**

This project was made possible through the generous financial support of James and Sharon Todd.

**ULI also wishes to acknowledge the following organizations for their help, support, and involvement with this effort:**

The Colorado Health Foundation, Denver, Colorado

The Center for Active Design, New York City

The University of Virginia School of Architecture, Center for Design and Health, Charlottesville, Virginia

Urban Land Institute

## About the Urban Land Institute

The mission of the Urban Land Institute is to provide leadership in the responsible use of land and in creating and sustaining thriving communities worldwide.

Established in 1936, the Institute today has nearly 30,000 members, representing the entire spectrum of land use and development disciplines. Professionals represented include developers, builders, property owners, investors, architects, planners, public officials, real estate brokers, appraisers, attorneys, engineers, financiers, academics, and students.

ULI is committed to

- ☐ Bringing together leaders from across the fields of real estate and land use policy to exchange best practices and serve community needs;
- ☐ Fostering collaboration within and beyond ULI's membership through mentoring, dialogue, and problem solving;
- ☐ Exploring issues of urbanization, conservation, regeneration, land use, capital formation, and sustainable development;
- ☐ Advancing land use policies and design practices that respect the uniqueness of both the built and natural environment;
- ☐ Sharing knowledge through education, applied research, publishing, and electronic media; and
- ☐ Sustaining a diverse global network of local practice and advisory efforts that address current and future challenges.

**Recommended bibliographic listing:**

Eitler, Thomas W., Edward T. McMahon, and Theodore C.Thoerig. *Ten Principles for Building Healthy Places.* Washington, D.C.: Urban Land Institute, 2013.

ISBN: 978-0-87420-283-0


1025 Thomas Jefferson Street, NW
Suite 500 West
Washington, DC 20007-5201



## About the Building Healthy Places Initiative

*Leveraging the power of ULI's global networks to shape projects and places in ways that improve the health of people and communities.*

Around the world, communities face pressing health challenges related to the built environment. For many years, ULI and its members have been active players in discussions and projects that make the link between human health and development; we know that health is a core component of thriving communities.

In January 2013, ULI's Board of Directors approved a focus on healthy communities as a cross-disciplinary theme for the organization. Through the Building Healthy Places Initiative, launched in late July 2013, ULI will work over two years to promote health in projects and places across the globe.

ULI is focusing on four main areas of impact:

- ☐ Awareness—raising awareness of the connections between health and the built environment in the real estate community and working to make sure health is a mainstream consideration;
- ☐ Tools—developing or widely sharing tools, including best practices, criteria, and other materials that define and advance approaches to healthy buildings, projects, and communities;
- ☐ Value—building understanding of the market and nonmarket factors at play in building healthy places and of the value proposition of building and operating in health-promoting ways; and
- ☐ Commitments—gaining commitments from members and others, including local governments, to work, build, and operate in more health-promoting ways.

Learn more and connect with Building Healthy Places at www.uli.org/health.

# Contents

# ULI Staff

## ULI Project Staff

**Thomas W. Eitler**
Vice President, Advisory Services

**Edward T. McMahon**
Senior Resident Fellow/Charles Fraser Chair for Sustainable Development and Environmental Policy

**Gayle Berens**
Senior Vice President, Education and Advisory Group

**Rachel MacCleery**
Senior Vice President, Content

**Basil Hallberg**
Senior Research Associate

**Alison Johnson**
Program Manager, ULI Rose Center for Public Leadership

**Graham Stroh**
Director, District Council Programs

**Kathryn Craig**
Associate, Education and Advisory Group

**Caroline Dietrich**
Logistics Manager, Advisory Services Program

**James Mulligan**
Senior Editor

**Laura Glassman**, Publications Professionals LLC
Manuscript Editor

**Betsy VanBuskirk**
Creative Director

**Craig Chapman**
Senior Director, Publishing Operations

## ULI Senior Executives

**Patrick Phillips**
Chief Executive Officer

**Cheryl Cummins**
Executive Officer

**Michael Terseck**
Chief Financial Officer/Chief Administrative Officer

**Lela Agnew**
Executive Vice President, Communications

**Kathleen B. Carey**
Executive Vice President/Chief Content Officer

**David Howard**
Executive Vice President, Development and ULI Foundation

**Joe Montgomery**
Chief Executive, Europe

**John Fitzgerald**
Chief Executive, Asia Pacific

**Marilee Utter**
Executive Vice President, District Councils

# Participants

## Chair

**David Scheuer**
President
The Retrovest Companies
Burlington, Vermont

## Workshop Participants

**Ellen Bassett**
Associate Professor, Urban and Environmental Planning
University of Virginia School of Architecture
Charlottesville, Virginia

**Mary Borgia**
President
The Borgia Company
Newport Beach, California

**Laura Burnett**
Principal
Burnett Land & Water
San Diego, California

**Suzanne Cameron**
Principal
Suzanne Cameron LLC
Washington, D.C.

**Debra Campbell**
Planning Director
Charlotte-Mecklenburg Planning Department
Charlotte, North Carolina

**Erin Christensen**
Associate Principal
Mithun
Seattle, Washington

**Joanna Frank**
Executive Director
Center for Active Design
New York, New York

**Brian T. Guenzel**
Director, Institute of Urban Studies
University of Texas at Arlington
Arlington, Texas

**Kamuron Gurol**
Director of Community Development
City of Sammamish
Sammamish, Washington

**Andrew Irvine**
Principal
RNL Design
Denver, Colorado

**Dr. Richard J. Jackson**
Professor/Chair, Environmental Health Sciences
UCLA Fielding School of Public Health
Los Angeles, California

**Debbie Lou**
Program Analyst
Active Living Research
San Diego, California

**Mary Lydon**
Executive Director
ULI San Diego/Tijuana

**Jana Lynott**
Senior Strategic Policy Adviser
PPI Livable Communities Team
AARP Inc.
Washington, D.C.

**James A. Moore**
Senior Vice President
HDR Inc.
Tampa, Florida

**Marja Preston**
President
Asani Development Corp.
Bainbridge Island, Washington

**Anna Ricklin**
Manager, Planning and Community Health Research Center
American Planning Association
Washington, D.C.

**Peter Rummell**
Rummell Company LLC
Jacksonville, Florida

**Brad Segal**
President
P.U.M.A
Denver, Colorado

**Ed Starkie**
Principal
Urban Advisors Ltd.
Portland, Oregon

**Bob Taunton**
President
Taunton Group LLC
Boise, Idaho

**Ross Tilghman**
Director
Tilghman Group
Seattle, Washington

**Tamara Zahn**
President
Zahn Associates
Indianapolis, Indiana

# Introduction

This is a publication about healthy places. Physical design affects human behavior at all scales—buildings, neighborhoods, communities, and regions. The places in which we live, work, and play can affect both our mental and physical well-being. Today, communities across the United States are facing obesity and chronic disease rates of epic proportions. Our built environment offers both opportunities for and barriers to improving public health and increasing active living. Communities designed in a way that supports physical activity—wide sidewalks, safe bike lanes, attractive stairways, accessible recreation areas—encourage residents to make healthy choices and live healthy lives. Healthy places in turn create economic value by attracting both younger and older workers and appeal to a skilled workforce and innovative companies.

One challenge to building healthy places is the lack of a common language between the medical and land use community. To that end, the Urban Land Institute convened a group of interdisciplinary experts at an August 5–6, 2013, workshop as part of its Building Healthy Places Initiative. The team—purposely drawn from a variety of fields and perspectives, including health care, architecture, planning, development, finance, academia, and research—was asked to develop ten principles for building healthy communities around the globe. Team members devoted two days of intensive study and collaboration, ultimately consolidating and refining their conclusions as the ten principles presented in this booklet.

In spring 2013, the Colorado Health Foundation commissioned three ULI Advisory Services panels with a specific focus on evaluating three communities with very different land use typologies. The three panels were held in Arvada (suburban), Lamar (rural), and Westwood in Denver (urban), thereby allowing ULI to compare and contrast local actions based on these different land use forms. The Colorado Health Foundation has been an excellent partner in exploring this important subject and was instrumental in ULI's decision to conduct this Ten Principles workshop.

Obesity and other health problems, including asthma, diabetes, and depression, have very real costs, according to Dr. Richard J. Jackson, chair of Environmental Health Sciences at UCLA's School of Public Health and former director of the National Center for Environmental Health of the U.S. Centers for Disease Control and Prevention (CDC). According to the CDC, health care expenditures in 2007 represented 16.7 percent of gross domestic product (GDP) and are projected to grow to 19 percent of GDP by 2017, said Jackson, quoted in the *Urban Land* article "Healthy Communities: A New Direction in Development." In 2010, more than one-third of adults in the United States and almost 17 percent of youths were obese. Medical costs associated with obesity were estimated at $147 billion per year; on average, annual medical costs for people who are obese were $1,429 higher than for individuals of normal weight.

*"We now know that developers can be more effective in achieving public health than the doctors in white coats."*
—Dr. Richard J. Jackson, chair of Environmental Health Sciences at UCLA's School of Public Health and former director of the CDC's National Center for Environmental Health

One of the more important determinants of physical activity is a person's immediate environment. Most people who live in neighborhoods with parks, trails, and greenways are twice as healthy as people who live in neighborhoods without such facilities, said Kimball Crangle, a senior developer with the Denver Housing Authority, quoted in the same *Urban Land* article, citing the *American Journal of Preventive Medicine* (http://activelivingresearch.org/files/Bedimo-Rung_AJPM_2005.pdf). Those who participate in regular physical activity experience lower mortality rates; lower risk for heart disease, stroke, and diabetes; and improvement in emotional well-being. Although people with more healthy lifestyles often seek out such locations, proximity and access to such areas for a wider segment of the population is likely to improve overall community health.

Changes in physical design over the past 50 years have led to lifestyle changes, which have led to health impacts. Once part of our normal lives, physical activity has been designed out of daily living. Desk jobs have taken the place of manual labor, driving has replaced walking and biking, elevators and escalators have

supplanted stair climbing, and television and video games have displaced outdoor recreation—especially among children. "There is a connection, for example, between the fact that the urban sprawl we live with daily makes no room for sidewalks or bike paths and the fact that we are an overweight, heart disease–ridden society," said Jackson.

Emerging research is increasingly making the connection between transit-rich communities and better health outcomes. A knowledge gap exists, however, between research and implementation, with health and land use practitioners uncertain of how to apply the mounting body of evidence that shows the relationship between our built environment and our health.

This gap represents a tremendous opportunity for the development community—if it is addressed properly. Today, ample evidence supports the idea that consumer demand for healthy communities—walkable, vibrant places designed around transit and green spaces—has never been higher. Numerous studies show that demand for compact, mixed-use, transit-accessible development far outstrips current supply. Walkable communities are in such high demand, in fact, that they achieve from 40 to 100 percent more than traditional, automobile-oriented communities in terms of sales and lease price.

Consumer demand for healthy communities is particularly prominent among millennials, a demographic that is increasingly rejecting the automobile-centric land use patterns of the generations before them. Integrating health into planning and development policy can become an economic development strategy—a tool to attract a skilled workforce and to build an innovative and sustainable economic base.

*Whether the setting is urban, suburban, or rural, the design of the physical environment affects residents' health.*

The development community now faces the challenge of making the healthy choice the easy and affordable one. The premium commanded by walkable, transit-oriented development could price out senior citizens, people with disabilities, or low-to-moderate-income individuals—the very groups most at risk for health problems. In small towns and rural areas not served by transit, creative low-cost tools to increase physical activity will be needed to promote healthy living.

This booklet sets out ten important principles that can be used to create a new approach to building healthy communities. It is an approach that will help people live longer, more productive lives, reduce unhealthy lifestyles, help improve a community's competitive advantages, and allow developers, investors, local governments, and citizens to prosper in the 21st century.

# Ten Principles for Building Healthy Places

1. **Put People First**
2. **Recognize the Economic Value**
3. **Empower Champions for Health**
4. **Energize Shared Spaces**
5. **Make Healthy Choices Easy**
6. **Ensure Equitable Access**
7. **Mix It Up**
8. **Embrace Unique Character**
9. **Promote Access to Healthy Food**
10. **Make It Active**

# 1 Put People First

## Individuals are more likely to be active in a community designed around their needs.

### Complete Streets Make Roads Better for Everyone

**Historically, traffic engineers took as their primary charge the need to move traffic swiftly and smoothly from one location to the next, with relatively little focus on pedestrians. Studies show that pedestrian injuries and deaths are more than twice as likely to occur in places without sidewalks, and more than 40 percent of pedestrian fatalities occur where no crosswalk is available.**

**Complete Streets is a transportation policy that provides safe access for all road users—pedestrians, cyclists, public transit users, and motorists—of all ages and abilities. It requires that transportation agencies routinely design and operate the entire right of way to enable safe access for all users and engage the public to identify the most desired and active transportation solutions. Although design features vary based on local context, basic elements should include wide sidewalks, well-marked or raised crosswalks, traffic-calming measures, protected bike lanes, and pedestrian safety islands.**

**To date, more than 500 jurisdictions in the United States have adopted a Complete Streets policy. Data from Charlotte, North Carolina, show that the cost of constructing a Complete Street was only 2.5 to 8 percent more than that of a traditional four-lane road with 12-foot-wide lanes—well within the normal annual variation in construction costs. Complete Streets can help reduce costs and improve health by significantly reducing crash rates, injuries, and fatalities. In addition, Complete Streets are often better designed than conventional streets, with features such as park strips, street trees, and street furniture that enhance economic opportunity and social interaction.**

For decades, planners and developers inadvertently designed places for cars, not people. The results—separation of uses, acres of parking, and long commutes. These have all contributed to the decline in our country's health. One of the strongest health/land use correlations is between obesity and the automobile: one California study showed each additional hour spent in a car per day is associated with a 6 percent increase in body weight, whereas every kilometer (0.6 miles) walked each day is associated with a 5 percent decrease, according to a study in British Columbia.

Similarly, educators say that an active student is a better learner. In the past, most children walked to school because schools were designed and located at the center of our neighborhoods. Today, however, only a very small percentage of children walk to school because we changed our school siting and design standards. Today, typical new elementary and high schools are located on the outskirts of our towns rather than in the center.

A healthy urban community is one where basic necessities and community amenities are accessible by walking or biking. Access to space for physical activity, such as walking paths and exercise facilities near work and home, is associated with increased physical activity, as is proximity to parks and playgrounds. Countries with strong bicycle infrastructure report higher levels of bicycle use and lower rates of obesity.

Building design significantly affects health as well. Recent health studies have linked increased stair use with better health outcomes: men who climbed three to five flights of stairs a day had a 29 percent lower risk of stroke. Daylight and views of nature are associated with reduced pain and depression, and high-quality air-ventilation systems are associated with lower incidence of respiratory disease and increased worker productivity.

- **A** Street Trees
- **B** Lighting
- **C** Furnishings
- **D** Materials and Finishes
- **E** Landscape Planters
- **F** Broad Sidewalks
- **G** On-Street Parking
- **H** Bicycle Lane
- **I** Narrow Travel Lanes
- **J** Textured Turn Lanes
- **K** Street Presence from Buildings

## Consider health upfront

Communities make decisions every day that affect public health; incorporating health early in decision making sets a community up for achieving strong results. Instead of being tacked on at the end, health should be incorporated intentionally at the outset of policy or investment decisions.

The first step toward building healthy places is creating a physical environment that encourages walking and other physical activity by everyone. But to create that environment, traffic engineers, schools boards, and land use regulators must prioritize people over cars.

## Integrate health into planning

Many communities adopt comprehensive plans, master plans, and general plans that local governments use to guide development and investment decisions. Cities, counties, and towns rely on their adopted comprehensive plan to evaluate development proposals and to focus public resources such as infrastructure, schools, parks, and libraries to best serve the public.

According to a 2011 survey by the American Planning Association, fewer than 10 percent of respondents said their plan explicitly addressed health conditions such as obesity prevention, and just 3 percent reported that their community's comprehensive plan had a stand-alone chapter addressing public health.

All comprehensive plans should incorporate health. It can even be included as a stand-alone chapter that is connected to more traditional plan sections. A stand-alone chapter provides the opportunity to make explicit the connection between development and health, to elevate health among planning considerations, and to lay the groundwork for a healthy community for generations to come. A broad spectrum of stakeholders should be engaged to create the vision for each healthy community and identify priority issues.

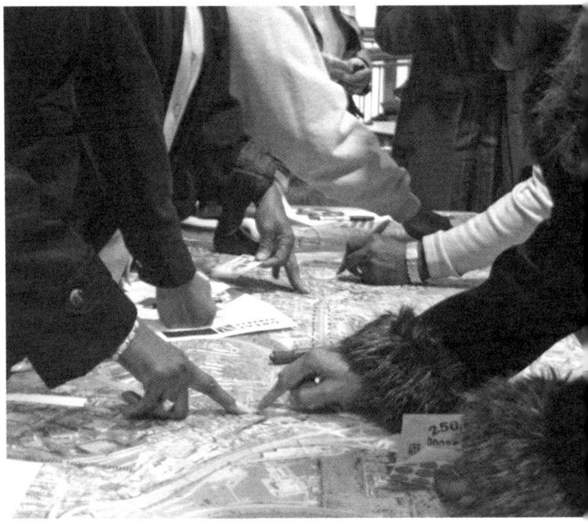

*Incorporating health into a community's public planning process lays the groundwork for a community for generations to come.*

## Consider health impacts

A health impact assessment (HIA) is another tool that considers health upfront. An HIA is a planning tool that helps evaluate the potential health effects of a plan, project, or policy before it is built or implemented. HIAs bring potential public health impacts and considerations to the decision-making process for plans, projects, and policies that fall outside the traditional public health arenas, such as transportation and land use. It is a "health lens" that can help increase positive health outcomes and minimize adverse health outcomes. San Francisco has been an early adopter of HIAs, using the tool on diverse projects, such as neighborhood plans, affordable housing, and highway projects.

The development community, local government, or both in cooperation can develop HIAs. Doctors advise their patients on how they can stay healthy, and in many ways, an HIA provides the same advice to communities. This guidance helps communities make informed choices about improving public health through community design.

# 2 Recognize the Economic Value

## Healthy places can create enhanced economic value for both the private and public sectors.

Recent demographic and lifestyle shifts show that consumers of all ages increasingly want to live in walkable, mixed-use, transit-rich communities. The economic downturn confirmed this trend: the places that best held their value were compact areas that offered mobility choices, local parks, and nearby retail and transit. Banks and insurers, once hesitant to underwrite unproven development models, are now increasingly aware of the value premium of these neighborhoods.

The preference shift toward healthy places and walkable communities represents an enormous opportunity for the development community. Compact, walkable communities provide economic benefits to developers through higher home sale prices, enhanced marketability, and faster sales or leases than conventional

### Walkable Retail Enlivens Complete Streets and Improves Economic Value

**In 2012, New York City's *Measuring the Street* report quantified the economic impact of safe, walkable, and more attractive streetscapes. Using a cross section of recent New York City Department of Transportation street design projects, the project found that Complete Street strategies such as protected bicycle lanes, pedestrian safety islands, new pedestrian plazas, and simplified intersections could reduce the number of vehicle and pedestrian accidents as well as raise commercial rents and retail sales.**

**These improvements served the dual purpose of strengthening the economic vitality of a neighborhood and allowing its citizens to be more physically active.**

**Walkable retail environments have been shown to have significant economic return. Automobile-dependent retail must depend on drive-by traffic alone, sacrificing leasable area for on-site parking. These businesses must have long frontages and large signs to be seen by drivers. The result for the investor is a product that must be quickly amortized; for the community, it is property of low community value and high traffic impact.**

development, according to a 2010 report by Active Living Research. These benefits accrue to healthy communities in suburban or rural locations as well, where developments that preserve land for open space, trails, and greenways have sold more quickly and often have a higher rate of presold units than conventional suburban developments.

Two of the largest and most sought-after market segments—millennials and baby boomers—are increasingly choosing vibrant, walkable communities. Since 2000, the number of college-educated 25- to 34-year-olds has increased twice as fast in the close-in neighborhoods of the nation's large cities than in the remainder of these metropolitan areas. Study after study shows that millennials place less value in cars or car ownership, instead spending money on shared experiences such as food, and music and art. A cycling culture has emerged among millennials, who make up the primary market of popular bike-share programs. The American Community Survey recently noted that the bicycle community grew by 10 percent between 2011 and 2012. In addition, when New York City opened registration for its bike-share program in April 2013, more than 5,000 people signed up on the first day.

Today, college graduates are clustering in America's most vibrant and active metropolitan areas. Active cities have become magnets for skilled workers and the millennial generation. Those cities' ability to attract and retain the highly skilled workforce coveted by the high-tech industry can in turn become a powerful economic development tool to recruit and retain innovative companies. In fact, these clusters of highly active knowledge workers are triggering new markets, new opportunities, and new products and services.

In a global economy where capital is footloose and the natural resources or geographic location of a city have become less important, a key concept for economic development has become community differentiation: in short, a community's unique appeal drives economic prosperity. A healthy community can provide economic advantage by appealing to millennials who, as a generation, place more value on active lifestyles, and older generation X families that are seeking a variety of amenities, such as parks, trails, and recreation, in which to raise their children.

The appeal also extends to baby boomers. Although surveys show that the majority of the 55- to 64-year-old demographic prefers to "age in place," those who do move increasingly want to live in areas where they can walk and bike to amenities such as restaurants, libraries, and cultural activities. Developers can create enduring value by meeting these demands all along the age curve.

The economic opportunity of healthy places is not limited to large cities. As the tide of the housing collapse recedes, many suburbs, small towns, and rural communities find themselves in competition with one another. Outer-ring communities that can reinvent themselves as healthy mixed-use places will gain a competitive advantage, using active living as a way to attract investment in the community, foster growth, and increase revenues. A healthy population can also reduce the cost of health care, safety, education, and operations.

# 3 Empower Champions for Health

## Every movement needs its champions.

Community engagement is a powerful vehicle for bringing about changes that improve the health of a community and its residents. But for many towns and cities, the connection between the built environment and personal health may not yet be apparent. A shared vision of a healthy community must take root before it can be cultivated and brought to bear on land development.

Passionate and respected leaders can bring credibility to the concept of building healthy places. This grassroots leadership is critical to attract resources and energy and to secure "buy-in" throughout the community. Selecting and cultivating the messenger, therefore, becomes as important as the message. Without respected leaders to elevate and promote the concept of healthy places across the stakeholder spectrum, the vision will not be achieved.

A number of strategies can be used to cultivate a shared vision of a healthy community:

- □ **Communicate the benefits.** Conveying the full scope of benefits—economic, social, and personal—of healthy places to all stakeholders is essential.

### Denver's Healthy Living Initiative Brings New Life to Mariposa

**The Denver Housing Authority (DHA) and its partners are in the process of redeveloping nearly 900 new mixed-income housing units in the Mariposa neighborhood near downtown Denver. Starting in 2009, the DHA and its master planning team, Seattle-based Mithun, established physical, mental, and community health as a proxy to understand how redevelopment actions would change the quality of life for residents. The initiative, designed to be a living implementation tool for designers, developers, and practitioners, uses a responsive and rigorous approach to address environmental and social determinants of health. Extensive public engagement helped identify the changes needed to make a healthier community. The process itself helped identify champions within the community.**

*Mariposa is an example of how champions such as the housing authority and the residents combined their efforts to achieve a positive outcome in terms of health. Together, they focused on building the Mariposa brand, encouraging grassroots actions, and communicating the benefits of an improved community.*

**The initiative set priority areas: increase physical activity; improve pedestrian and bike opportunities; increase mobility and traffic safety; improve access to healthy foods; increase safety and security; and improve access to health care. The team, using a health measurement tool, established services to help improve health determinants for residents and policies that incentivize healthy behavior and opportunities.**

**Monitoring has shown positive trends in many of the indicators of a healthy community, such as the total crime rate, which has dropped from 246 crimes per 1,000 people in 2005, to 157 in 2011, or the average transit commute time, which has dropped from 24 minutes in 2010 to 20 minutes in 2012. In the first phase of development, Tapiz, a 100-unit multifamily building, several elements were incorporated to improve health of residents, such as an eight-story building-integrated mural that celebrates the cultural diversity and history of the neighborhood and the community gardens available to residents to grow their own fresh foods in partnership with Denver Urban Gardens.**

Champions must ask themselves: How will each segment of the community benefit? Will these changes bring economic vitality; help our children; improve resilience, jobs, and revenue? Will they create an environment that attracts young and working families? Will they improve the choices of people with low or moderate incomes, persons with disabilities, or senior citizens?

- ☐ **Encourage grassroots action.** The business case for healthy communities is a powerful motivator for both private and public sector leadership and the policies they will adopt. However, creating and sustaining healthy places requires a bottom-up approach. Community members must be identified and empowered to lead the effort, identify areas of need, set priorities, and take part in implementation. Leadership must come from the local community—business owners, health practitioners, community organizers, or faith-based leaders—rather than just the government in order to build credibility. Grassroots champions must value collaboration, represent a diverse array of community interests, and be unafraid to take action and learn from it.

- ☐ **Broaden the base.** Cultivating a vision of health and wellness requires early, frequent, and broad public participation. Champions must be careful not to isolate target audiences; rather, the language and message must appeal to a broad mix of ages, races, and incomes. Active living may be an opportunity to engage younger, less traditionally involved demographics who value health as a lifestyle choice. Creating a broad base of constituents is not easy: it often requires building trust between groups that may not have a history of working together.

- ☐ **Build a brand.** Health is an aspirational and, ultimately, personal issue—everyone cares about their personal well-being and that of their loved ones. Extending that personal concept of wellness to the community level is a powerful branding opportunity. A communication plan should focus on educating people about the importance of engaging in healthy activities and programs, ultimately creating a sense of neighborhood or community identity around an active lifestyle.

- ☐ **Forge unlikely partnerships.** Historically, doctors and developers have had little reason to collaborate. As the connection between land use and health becomes well understood, partnerships that merge development and health interests should be formed. The Colorado Health Foundation, for example, recently invited a prominent group of real estate professionals, including developers, architects, and planners, to help design a new "health-positive" building for the foundation's headquarters. Similarly, Cooper Green Mercy Hospital in Birmingham, Alabama, recently created a partnership between doctors and nurses, and local contractors, landscape architects, public officials, and former patients to create an organic community garden in an underserved neighborhood near the hospital. In the future, many more opportunities will no doubt arise for partnerships between the development and public health communities.

# 4 Energize Shared Spaces

## Public gathering places have a direct, positive impact on human health.

Places with high levels of social isolation, which can be exacerbated by the lack of public spaces and transit options, are correlated with declines in well-being and higher health costs. Loneliness, depression, and anxiety can stem from social isolation. Symptoms can affect those of any age, but often older adults are particularly vulnerable because of the loss of friends and family and their own mobility challenges.

A healthy community is one that engages all its residents. Vibrant community places can offer opportunities for people to socialize with their friends and family as well as engage with people they might not otherwise meet. A well-designed public and semi-public realm can foster this serendipitous social interaction, and good programming can draw people out of their homes and into their community.

### Map community assets

A scan conducted across the community and region can identify existing assets and gaps related to opportunities for physical activity and social engagement. This mapping process can document areas of need and help target and prioritize capital improvements and programs; for instance, a survey of vacant downtown land can identify sites for temporary public space.

### Take back the street

The residential street should be regarded as a primary public space, not merely a conduit to meet travel needs. Communities should use the "living street" concept where appropriate. A living street is a street primarily designed for pedestrians and cyclists and a social space where people can meet and children can play safely and legally. This does not mean that vehicles cannot use the street. It means that vehicular access is subordinated to pedestrian use. Living streets can reclaim public space for community and commercial activity, and in some cases they have been shown to increase storefront rents. For smaller or less urban communities, a temporary living street can be a solution, for example, closing select streets to traffic on Sunday afternoons. Best practices include the following:

- ☐ Zero-grade separation between sidewalk and street right-of-way creates a plazalike feel.
- ☐ Wide sidewalks accommodate both pedestrian and retail activity.
- ☐ Trees, planters, and public art slow cars and make streets more attractive for shoppers and pedestrians.
- ☐ Active and at-grade ground-floor uses and street furniture create an inviting and accessible atmosphere.
- ☐ Gateway treatments, removal of striping, and pavement changes announce a low-speed environment.

### New York City Creates Pedestrian Plazas from Street Space

**Streets make up about 25 percent of New York City's land area, and yet, outside of parks, streets provide few places to sit, rest, socialize, and enjoy public life. To improve the quality of life for New Yorkers and create more opportunities for social engagement, the city created more public open space by reclaiming underused street space and transforming it into pedestrian plazas.**

**To date, the city has 26 new plazas that are in some phase of planning, design, or construction, with three additional plazas expected each year for the next ten years. The most high-profile pedestrian plazas are improving quality of life and safety for New Yorkers and visitors. A prime example is Times Square, where the city and the business improvement district are preparing to make permanent the public space enhancements that were installed as part of a six-month pilot during the summer of 2009.**

**Communities large and small have underused or leftover spaces along central intersections or corridors. Creating pop-up plazas can be a low-cost solution to fostering social engagement and enlivening public space.**

*A Public Plaza Plan for underused space in New York City.*

## Rethink public places

Ample and flexible space of all sizes should be available for public gathering. Most parks should not be passive, single-use recreation areas. Some cities are creating pop-up parks to enliven underused public spaces. A pop-up park is a temporary use of vacant or underused space: a parking lot can become a farmers market; an urban square that is a lunch spot by day can host concerts or outdoor films at night. Programming, often through a dedicated manager or business improvement district (BID), helps keep the public spaces active and inviting at all times and in all seasons.

*Pop-up parks are temporary public spaces that allow cities to test-drive new concepts for public spaces. Examples of possible activities include play streets, movies in the park, yoga classes, food streets, art festivals, chess tournaments, and soapbox lectures. The concept behind pop-up parks is to explore which activities best suit the citizens of a particular area and how those activities can energize these public spaces, thereby leading to a more healthy local population.*

## Program early and often

Improvements to the built environment can take years to bring to fruition and require substantial capital investment; programming is often a quick and inexpensive solution that can produce instant results. Simple programming, such as street festivals, health fairs, and athletic events, can get people outside and into the community. Social engagement can be both spontaneous and planned, but in most cases, to sustain social interaction, spaces must be energized and programmed.

## Explore fail-fast initiatives

Because of the inexpensive nature of programming, localities should not be afraid to try new ideas and tactics, some of which may end in failure. Pilot projects or spontaneous interventions—such as San Francisco's Park(ing) Day, where artists and designers occupy metered parking spaces for a day, transforming them into a temporary public space—can serve as test cases at the local level. While Park(ing) Day was a success, other similar projects may fail. Failure should not be punished, merely discovered early and fixed quickly.

## Encourage public/private cooperation

Because community places involve a mix of public and private realms, cooperation between property owners and local government is crucial. Public/private partnerships, often in the form of BIDs, are necessary to finance programs and recruit vendors for business opportunities. Existing regulations often need to be amended to allow temporary use permits or rezone land to permit mixed-use activities. Community foundations or nonprofit organizations can offer mini-grants to jump-start grassroots or pilot programming. Also, public school partnerships with local government and private organizations regarding curriculums, fresh-food production, and in-school consumption should be explored.

# 5 Make Healthy Choices Easy

## Communities should make the healthy choice the one that is SAFE—safe, accessible, fun, and easy.

Prevailing land use practices often present real and perceived barriers to change. Planning and design can create the hardware—cleaner, safer, more beautiful streets with a variety of transportation options—to overcome the physical barriers to an active lifestyle. And programming—easy, fun, and inclusive opportunities available to all—can serve as the software to surmount the perceptions that keep people from changing their behavior.

Health is about individual choices. To overcome inertia—after all, human nature is to do what is easy and what one knows—communities must make the healthy option the easy option. By providing a menu of choices that are easy and accessible to all, a community can lower the barriers to entry for an active life. For example, if you want children to walk to school, make sure they have sidewalks and safe pedestrian crossings between their neighborhoods and schools.

When planning their communities, practitioners should ask themselves the following questions.

### Do people feel safe?

Traffic conditions or poor street design can deter the hardiest cyclist, let alone a novice biker. And dimly lit and dirty streets can feel unsafe and uninviting to pedestrians. The National Association of City Transportation Officials has guidelines for designing safe bicycle and pedestrian facilities that can help foster a safe and secure environment. Key elements include the following:

- ☐ Sidewalks designed with appropriate width, lighting, shade, trees, buffers from moving vehicles, street furniture, and public art;
- ☐ Bikeways and bike crossings at intersections well marked for maximum visibility;
- ☐ Bikeways protected from traffic through striping, planters, street parking, and curbs;
- ☐ Refuges for pedestrians through raised and buffered islands at wide or complex intersections; and
- ☐ Raised planter boxes or bollards as temporary and low-cost solution for unsafe or unattractive areas.

*The National Association of City Transportation Officials'* Urban Bikeway Design Guide *provides numerous options for bikeways, focusing on safe and efficient sharing of public roadways.*

### How accessible are the transportation options?

Can people walk to their destinations? Can they bike to them? Can they use transit? How many users would reasonably have these choices?

### The Indianapolis Cultural Trail Leads the Way

**The Indianapolis Cultural Trail is an eight-mile protected bike and pedestrian path that connects downtown Indianapolis with a half-dozen emerging cultural and entertainment districts. A 1.5-mile portion runs along the restored Indianapolis Canal, and alongside the path are sidewalks and swales designed to capture and filter stormwater runoff and to provide greenery and shade. Custom-designed benches, signs, and trash receptacles, along with extensive public art, contribute to the overall impression of safety, beauty, and quality.**

**The city timed a major programming rollout—a downtown-wide effort to stage 75 cultural and entertainment events along the trail—to coincide with the trail's May 2013 opening.**

**The $55 million trail was made possible through a combination of federal funds and philanthropic donations. The previously automobile-dominated city hopes the trail will play a major role in talent attraction and retention for the region and significantly improve economic development and quality of life in central Indiana.**

Healthy communities provide multiple, often overlapping, means of addressing key needs and providing key services. Roads carry cars, buses, transit, bicyclists, and pedestrians in a safe and equitable manner; very few travel elements are purely mono-functional. This approach reduces the costs to provide infrastructure and services and enhances the utility of systems by ensuring backups. To pursue this approach, do the following:

- ☐ Assess gaps and areas of mono-functional travel service through asset mapping.
- ☐ Develop pedestrian and biking plans that promote connectivity to a regional transit system.
- ☐ Improve and make clear local bus access to and from regional stations.

*Can we get more people to do the healthy thing by making it fun? Installed in 2009 at a subway stairwell in Stockholm, Sweden, as a fun musical experience for pedestrians, the original Piano Stairs project succeeded in attracting 66 percent more pedestrians to use the stairs instead of the escalator.*

*(The project's success was described by the RGK Center for Philanthropy and Community Service of the University of Texas at Austin.)*

## Will the experience of getting there be fun and interesting?

Public art and whimsical design can encourage people to walk and bicycle, creating a memorable and positive experience. Varied color, material, and signage can double as wayfinding devices and differentiate neighborhoods or communities. Enhancing and emphasizing beauty can be a key source of community pride and social cohesion.

The intangible benefits of public art—aesthetic beauty, cultural interpretation, education, inspiration, and general improvement of the urban environment—are apparent to us all. But the tangible benefits are less known. If done right, investing in public art can generate publicity, public recognition, and marketing cachet, a potential source of positive financial returns for property owners.

## Will it be easy?

Newcomers as well as existing residents may be unaware of community amenities or confused about directions or routes. Mass transit and bus systems can often be daunting for the uninitiated. Address wayfinding needs and develop a system of signage for pedestrians and cyclists. Neighborhood gateway markers, with appropriate scaled signage or public art, can orient people and strengthen neighborhood identity.

# 6 Ensure Equitable Access

## Many segments of the population would benefit from better access to services, amenities, and opportunities.

For school-age children, seniors on fixed incomes, people with disabilities, and those with social and economic disadvantages, the healthy choice is not always the easiest choice. Racial and ethnic minorities and low-income individuals tend to face greater disease burdens and have shorter lifespans than their nonminority and wealthier counterparts. The physical isolation and lack of access suffered by older people and those with disabilities are linked to early death and disease, and chronic exposure to stress may exacerbate these health disparities.

Increasing access to healthier living choices among these groups should not be seen as a cost burden. Designing for a variety of abilities and ages, especially in light of America's aging population, can generate value from both a real estate and a community health perspective. In the next 40 years, the number of Americans over the age of 65 will double from 40 million to 80 million. From 2010 to 2030, the number of U.S. homeowners over 65 will increase 70 percent, and the number of renters of the same age will increase 100 percent. The current lack of housing catering to the growing numbers in the older population segments represents a tremendous potential market for residential developers.

Improving the location and design of both public schools and affordable housing can also have very real benefits in terms of health costs and public expenditure. Low-income residents who often feel unsafe in their neighborhoods may be less likely to walk or exercise, and those in substandard housing may be exposed to poor air quality and environmentally hazardous materials like asbestos or lead paint. Areas near current or planned public transit stations represent a particularly favorable opportunity to integrate new affordable units by taking advantage of cross-subsidization opportunities presented by the rising demand and cost premium for transit-oriented development.

### Design for all ages and abilities

Universal design principles can and should be used to ensure access for all while accommodating the market realities of the aging curve. Sixty to 70 percent of Americans say they want to age in place, either in their current home or in their neighborhood. But most homes and communities are not set up to house the older population. A healthy community is a sustainable community—one where a person who is 20, 40, 60, or even 80 can live without any loss in quality of life. The Center for Universal Design at North Carolina State University publishes a set of principles for designing for all ages and abilities. They include the following:

- Equitable in use: open floor plans; first-floor bedrooms; stepless entries; easy-entry showers, handrails, and grab bars; higher electrical outlets; lower light switches;
- Flexible in use: adjustable countertops and shelves; varied cabinet heights; redundant systems that use both audio and video displays;
- Intuitive to use: pebbled or textured walkways; high-contrast color and surface texture schemes; and

Bird Watching along the Lamar Canal

Walking to School along the Fort Bent Canal

- ☐ Easy to use: components that require less than five pounds of force; easy-open hinges for doors and cabinets; lever handles rather than doorknobs.

## Integrate land use and transit

Prosperous and sustainable communities deploy adequate infrastructure to support all modes of travel, connecting all people to services and amenities. A transportation plan should focus on moving people, not cars, and include a wide array of stakeholders to ensure that transit needs are met. The more travel choices that are available to at-risk groups, the more likely they can pick the healthy choice.

In automobile-dependent communities, providing choice can be difficult. Many suburbs lack the density to support light rail or subway systems and may feature only limited bus service. For those places, connectivity is paramount: a complete sidewalk system, safe bicycle and pedestrian connections, and clear routes to safe and clean bus stations can increase travel choice.

Similarly, school siting and design decisions can have both economic and health impacts. Schools in walkable settings require smaller school transportation expenditures and allow more children to get exercise walking to and from school. This is particularly important today because many school districts have eliminated physical education from their curriculum.

A holistic transit plan will succeed only if it is accompanied by supportive land uses. For example, Charlotte, North Carolina, has for years linked its transportation and land use policies to create a regional transit vision. Focusing on its five major transportation corridors, the city implemented community-responsive mass-transit solutions—rapid bus transit to the southeast, light rail to the south, commuter rail to the north—that were paired with an investment strategy and regulatory framework to encourage development around future transit stations.

## Focus on schools

Public schools are a place where health disparities across income levels can be addressed. Public schools have increasingly been built on large sites away from the residential neighborhoods they serve. This trend is a significant predictor of how children travel to school: a study of South Carolina schools shows that students are four times more likely to walk to schools built before 1983 than those built after that date. Schools can be the center of a neighborhood not just for families with school-age children, but for all residents if the school also serves as a community center and recreation center.

## Lamar Loop

**A walk down Main Street in Lamar, Colorado, with a late winter storm blowing in tells a lot about the challenges of trying to exercise in this rural city on the southeastern Colorado plains. Conditions may include 50-mile-per-hour sandstorms, 18-wheelers blasting past at similar speeds, and for pedestrians, a dangerous situation caused by the lack of sidewalks, bike lanes, and safe crossings on this five-lane roadway, which also serves as U.S. Highway 50/287.**

**"The biggest barrier we hear about is the inability to walk or bike to work, to home, or to the grocery store," said Karen Bryant, chief operating officer of the Prowers Medical Center and a member of Lamar's Healthy Places Steering Committee. "There's nothing connecting the north and south sides of town. You have to cross the railroad tracks."**

**When completed, the Lamar Loop will be a seven-mile multiuse loop trail for walking, biking, and equestrian use as a central organizing feature that would connect the north side's Escondido Park and the south side's parks and recreation facilities to an existing greenway along the west side and an existing canal trail on the east side of the city. The rural town promotes the use of the trail as a safe route to school and work, as well as for city events and sports activities.**

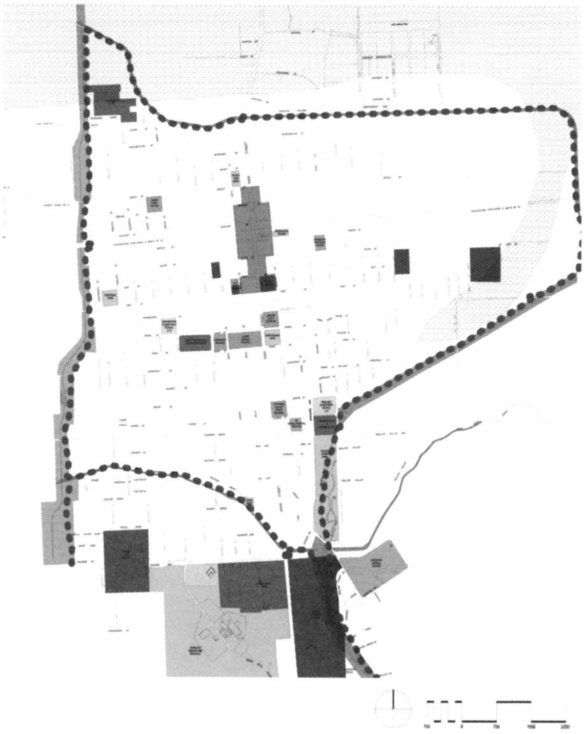

PEDESTRIAN ACCESS STRATEGY

# 7 Mix It Up

## A variety of land uses, building types, and public spaces can be used to improve physical and social activity.

Mixed-use development is any development or building that physically or functionally integrates a combination of residential, office, commercial, cultural, or institutional uses.

ULI has concluded that mixed-use development makes people much more likely to walk or use transit to run errands, go shopping, or go to lunch than does spread-out, automobile-oriented, single-use development. Researchers have found that even a base minimum of physical activity can help combat obesity. A simple walk to the transit stop or bus station can do wonders: a study of transit-oriented neighborhoods in Charlotte, North Carolina, found that light-rail users weighed on average six pounds less than those who do not use light rail. People are more likely to walk to destinations such as home, transit, shopping, or restaurants if these places are located within a quarter-mile to half-mile of their workplace.

Our land use patterns, however, often encourage a lifestyle where our only walk is from our home to the car in the driveway or from the parking garage to work. A dense and fine-grain mix of uses can support a variety of transportation options that increase access to essential goods and services and reduce health and environmental costs. In communities where this density is not possible, developers and planners can avoid monoculture by designing flexibility into the built environment and concentrating development in nodes.

Mixed-use development has dimensions beyond land use. Healthy places also mix incomes, generations, and housing type. This requires creative public/private partnerships: communities with a broad mix of housing and incomes, particularly around transit, often require incentives or financing programs to attain economic feasibility. ULI has encouraged the development of mixed-use centers in documents including *Ten Principles for Reinventing America's Suburban Strips* and *Ten Principles for Successful Development around Transit*.

One challenge to "mixing it up" is that the real estate industry tends toward simplicity: developers often prefer buildings to contain either a single use or at minimum a strong leading use. Some lenders are hesitant to finance unproven concepts, especially vertical mixed use, and municipalities have not always had success trying to regulate the mix of uses—for instance, requiring ground-floor retail where the market may not support it. How can towns and cities overcome these challenges?

*CityPlace in West Palm Beach, Florida, combines higher-density residential space with main-street retailing and active public gathering places.*

## Incentivize the mix

Local governments should match incentives to areas that lack certain amenities. Other tools to entice desired mixes and densities include floor/area ratio bonuses; affordable housing bonuses; density exclusions or tax abatements for preferred uses, such as a grocery stores or daycare centers; tax abatements; and impact-based development fees, among others.

## Remove regulatory barriers

Outdated zoning ordinances and building codes can deter mixed-use development even if planning guidance recommends it. For example, many zoning codes do not allow accessory dwelling units, which increase density, offer more housing options, and encourage intergenerational and mixed-income environments. Localities should update the regulatory framework to attract the right mix of development.

*A multigenerational mixed-use community located near Portland, Oregon, Bridge Meadows is designed to bring together three generations to support families adopting children from foster care and to create an opportunity for older residents to have a sense of community and purpose. Bridge Meadows works at the intersection of child welfare, aging, and affordable housing issues that affect each of us, not just socially and emotionally, but economically as well.*

## Rethink parking

Parking often makes the difference between smart growth and sprawl. But the problem of parking demand remains an important lever in the development process: too little parking leads to lost revenue; too much parking can raise the cost of housing or office rents. Communities large and small should revisit their parking policies to achieve the right balance. The city of Sacramento's parking ordinance, for instance, divides the city into areas based on parking need and eliminates parking minimums in transit-rich areas. The use of "district parking," where developers pay a fee in lieu of providing parking spaces, can provide centralized parking for multiple users and frees valuable ground for development as well as social interaction and recreational activities.

## Optimize uses

Retail uses should have high bay space and be configured to engage and enliven the public environment; residences at upper levels should be designed to be livable with appropriate privacy and amenities; office components should have a clear address and identity; public spaces should be flexible and programmed. No use should seem secondary, no matter its footprint.

# 8 Embrace Unique Character

## Places that are different, unusual, or unique can be helpful in promoting physical activity.

In 2010, the Knight Foundation partnered with the Gallup organization to survey 43,000 residents of 26 U.S. cities to determine what attracts people to a place and keeps them there. The study found that the most important factors that create emotional bonds between people and their communities were not jobs, but rather "physical beauty, opportunities for socializing, and a city's openness to all people." The Knight Foundation also found that communities with the highest levels of attachment to place also had the strongest economies. Cohesive communities also report higher levels of safety and security, community activity, and emotional health and well-being. Community involvement and political participation are associated with improved health outcomes; for instance, one study found a direct link between group membership and reduced mortality rates.

Often, the unique features that contribute to a deep-rooted sense of place are ecological, architectural, historic, or geographic. Proximity to natural places has a direct, positive effect on physical and mental health, as well as stress reduction. Studies have shown that children, in particular, have higher rates of physical activity the closer they live to parks and green space and report lower levels of stress and adversity.

### Greenville Uncovers the Falls on the Reedy

**The Reedy River Falls once powered Greenville, South Carolina's early grist mills, bringing industry and growth to the city. But by the mid-20th century, the river had become polluted by upstream textile mills, its banks littered with debris and trash. In 1960, a four-lane vehicular bridge was constructed over and across the falls, obstructing views and blocking public access to one of the city's most treasured natural features.**

*Falls Park on the Reedy.*

**Using funds generated through a local hospitality tax, the vehicular bridge was removed and the $13 million Falls on the Reedy Park opened in 2004. The park, located just off Main Street in the heart of downtown and within walking distance for many of the city's 19,000 workers, boasts a seamless alignment of architecture, art, and nature. The park is anchored by its most distinctive feature: the Liberty Bridge, a curving pedestrian bridge that spans 355 feet across the river, giving pedestrians unobstructed views of the falls below.**

**Falls Park also plays a prominent role in Greenville's growth and quality of life. It helped accelerate development along the Reedy River, forging the West End Historic District and sparking multiple mixed-use projects, and generated private investment in the immediate area, as evidenced by the $65 million RiverPlace mixed-use development, incorporating residential, office, restaurant, retail, and hotel uses and located directly across Main Street from the park. In addition, a new $29 million mixed-use baseball stadium, residential, office, restaurant, and retail development came online after the park's opening.**

**Greenville leaders often emphasize that success can be found in the special attributes of a community. Although that particular attribute is different in each city—in Greenville's case, it was a 60-foot waterfall located right off Main Street—capitalizing on those existing assets is crucial for economic development.**

Embracing the unique character of a site, neighborhood, or community can economically differentiate a project or place in the market, supporting asset value and bestowing a competitive advantage. The concept of authenticity is a slippery one, and artificial attempts to create it are often rejected by consumers. The following are some successful strategies for crafting a unique identity.

The Yards Park on the Anacostia River blends active and passive activities with the heritage of an industrial waterfront.

## Rediscover assets

Many towns and cities have had success by rediscovering their waterfronts or historic neighborhoods. Washington, D.C.'s initiative to reclaim the Anacostia River, for example, has resulted in more than $7 billion in private investment in neighborhoods, offices, and parks near the river.

A community-driven process can help identify the key assets of a place and prioritize development. Special characteristics can be identified, celebrated, and expressed through programming, art, and design, thus creating a focal point upon which to build community identity. A strong communication plan can translate the economic and health benefits to residents, developers, and decision makers.

## Integrate natural systems

Connecting to nature often means reconnecting natural features or environments, such as native forests or streams that may have been cut off by development or paved over. A healthy natural environment can reduce costs and contribute to the quality of life for residents, workers, and visitors. Smaller cities such as Greenville, South Carolina, have had great success: the city's Falls Park on the Reedy—a winding downtown park that uncovered a waterfall that for decades was covered by a concrete overpass—has helped generate more than $100 million in downtown investment.

Cities and towns should link new investment to its benefits for natural ecosystems and use it to prioritize development. This strategy applies at all scales—from a simple bench under a tree, to an open window in the office, to a countywide reduction in greenhouse gases. A broad and consistent effort contributes to a unique feel of a community.

# 9 Promote Access to Healthy Food

## Because diet affects human health, access to healthy food should be a considered as part of any development proposal.

When considering what constitutes a healthy community, planners and developers have often failed to assign food the same prominence as transit, open space, or housing mix. When food does enter the conversation, it is often in a fragmented way—where a restaurant should be located or how to attract a grocery store tenant, for example. The role of healthy food in our communities, however, is much more comprehensive: it is a real estate amenity, community builder, and project differentiator.

Building healthy communities starts with physical access to food. Many inner-city and rural families have little to no access to fresh, healthy, or affordable foods. For example, Detroit, a city of 139 square miles, has just five grocery stores. Although Detroit may be an extreme case, many poor inner-city neighborhoods have long been underserved by full-service grocery stores. Likewise, residents of rural areas, some in the most productive agricultural regions of the country, are often 25 to 50 miles from the nearest full-service supermarket. The distance to the nearest supermarket or grocery store has been found by studies to predict healthier eating and lower risk of obesity and chronic disease.

But access to healthy food goes beyond a brick-and-mortar problem. Communities should strive to integrate the full spectrum of healthy food cultivation, retailing, and consumption into everyday life.

*Fresh Moves mobile produce market in Chicago brings affordable, healthy food to neighborhoods that cannot initially support a full-service grocery store.*

### Rethink the grocery store

The assumption of most planners and developers—that trips to the grocery store are infrequent, driving is the only mode of travel, and the amount of goods purchased requires the use of a car—dominates the economics of grocery retailers. Supermarkets, it is thought, require large physical footprints and even larger market areas to support them. In 2007, the Food Marketing Institute noted that the median grocery store size was 47,500 square feet.

A growing body of research, however, is showing that these assumptions may no longer be valid. A University of Washington study has discovered that more and more shoppers are traveling by foot or by bicycle and that shoppers are making more visits and buying fewer items on each visit. Other studies indicate that the retail model is "fracturing"—more consumers are shopping for groceries online or in nontraditional or fresh-format stores.

Developers and planners should rethink the modern grocery store in light of changing consumer patterns. In some Chicago neighborhoods, for example,

the grocery store can come to you: Fresh Moves, a mobile food market, uses a converted Chicago Transit Authority bus to offer fresh food, often at prices more affordable than retail chains located in affluent neighborhoods, to urban areas underserved by traditional groceries.

## Make food a destination

In major cities, historic markets have become destinations for food, both creating economic development opportunities and encouraging healthy eating. Food is a place-making tool for neighborhood and ethnic identity. The Ferry Building in San Francisco draws more than 1 million visitors a year and generates $1,250 per square foot. Detroit's Eastern Market 360 program is turning a historic marketplace into a community development anchor, addressing food access, workforce training, and job creation.

Outside urban areas, agricultural parks, food belts, and preservation districts can promote a history of agriculture and take advantage of growing awareness and popularity of farm-to-table food. In Maryland's Montgomery County, county officials match aspiring farmers with unused land in its Agriculture Reserve, returning the land to productivity and linking urban and rural areas.

## Incorporate access to healthy food into local land use and economic policy

Communities small and large should invest in natural lands, just as they identify where to invest in development. Cities and close-in suburbs can institute urban agricultural policies and allow vacant land to be used for community gardens. Community centers can be retrofitted with enhanced kitchen facilities to enable community cooking or nutrition programs. Less dense areas, especially those with a farming past, can create agricultural preservation districts that preserve open space and arable land. By promoting agricultural tourism and rediscovering their agrarian history, communities can further differentiate themselves and engage diverse populations through the sustainable agriculture movement.

## Detroit's Eastern Market Turns 360 Degrees

**In 2008, a full renovation of Detroit's Eastern Market was commissioned by the city. The master plan went beyond the physical rebuilding of the 1891 market, envisioning a dynamic food hub that would serve as a community development engine for the city and help "relocalize" the region's food system.**

**The plan, known as Eastern Market 360, adopted the food cycle as its model, using production, processing, and retail sale of food as a way to teach nutrition, train workers, and create new jobs in a distressed community. The program includes plans for a 2.5-acre "starter" greenhouse to seed community gardens throughout the city, a commissary for local mobile markets, classroom space for nutrition education and use by local schools, and an incubator kitchen for local food-related processing or catering businesses.**

**The ultimate goal of the program is to create a new local economy in Detroit, leveraging the market to create a robust food district that strengthens local communities through job creation and access to healthy food. The city estimates that recapturing just 20 percent of food production from areas outside the city would generate more than 4,000 jobs and $19 million in tax revenue.**

# 10 Make It Active

## Urban design can be employed to create an active community.

*Physical activity has almost been completely designed out of everyday life.*

In the time since its widespread adoption in the 1950s, the automobile has completely reorganized the land use patterns of the United States. Physical activity was designed almost completely out of everyday life. Social commentator Walter Lippmann once said: "We have changed the environment more quickly than we know how to change ourselves."

Communities should strive to create environments that encourage healthy lifestyles and maximize the opportunities for all residents to get the physical activity they need to stay healthy. Decisions regarding the built environment should always include consideration for making the physical improvements consistent with active design. The CDC recommends that adults need 150 minutes of moderate aerobic activity a week; children need even more—at least one hour of physical activity each day. Less than half of adults and children, however, meet those baseline requirements.

### Colocate activities

Recreational opportunities should provide universal appeal. For instance, provide adult exercise equipment or walking tracks near children's playgrounds to offer an opportunity for parents and guardians to exercise while they are supervising their children. Senior center activities could be colocated with libraries and schools, taking advantage of older adults' experience and time to engage in educational opportunities for children.

Access to safe neighborhood play spaces for children is associated with higher rates of physical activity and lower rates of time spent watching television and

*Adding colors to playgrounds encourages activity.*

*The High Line in New York City provides both active and passive amenities for residents and visitors.*

playing video games. Colocation can be used at offices as well: workplace physical activity programs in the United States have been shown to reduce short-term sick leave and health care costs and to increase productivity.

## Begin every trip with a walk

Prioritize walking and biking as safe, viable, and enjoyable modes of transportation and recreation throughout the community. A New York City initiative, for example, is a plan to ensure that all New Yorkers live within a ten-minute walk of a park. The city also is incorporating active design ideas—encouraging stair use and colocating recreation areas—into the request for proposals process.

## Implement active-living guidelines

Studies show that vehicle-pedestrian traffic accidents are more than twice as likely to occur in places without sidewalks, and more than 40 percent of pedestrian fatalities occur where no crosswalk is available. Active-living design guidelines can help fill gaps in the pedestrian and bicycle network to create a continuous, interconnected system. Regional bike plans and bike sharing can help promote contiguous access and enhance multimodal transportation.

*Successful bike-share programs have become increasingly popular, providing urban dwellers and visitors with an alternative, healthy option in transportation.*

## Design for flexibility

Land efficiency should be maximized for human engagement. The era of single-use districts and public buildings is over: multifunctional is the future. This is especially true in suburban or rural areas, where single-use buildings cannot be justified in a time of tight capital budgets. School buildings, sports facilities, and playgrounds should be open to the public through scheduled programming and for appropriate informal use. This joint use of public facilities may require rethinking of code or local laws to promote active lifestyles.

# Conclusion

Supported by current demographic and socioeconomic trends, market demand in cities, suburbs, and rural areas is undergoing fundamental shifts in response to concerns about community health. Today, physical inactivity and unhealthy diet are second only to tobacco use as the main causes of premature death in the United States. A growing body of research indicates that properly designed buildings, appropriate placement of structures, easy-to-reach parks, programming of community spaces, and access to healthy foods can have an extraordinary impact on community health. Communities need to leverage their health advantage and reimagine how property is developed and how people live so they can stay competitive and relevant.

Although it would be gratifying if all the preceding suggestions were adopted by every community, movement toward even a few would be beneficial. Many communities consider using "baby steps" or one step at a time. This incremental adoption of one or a few principles that are digestible and actionable would improve the community's appetite for more.

It is also important to understand that any community has many moving parts and that different constituencies can expect to benefit in different ways from these Ten Principles. The local government benefits because local economic development improves, the developer and investor benefit because they can create viable projects and add value, and the individual citizen benefits because the physical and cultural environment becomes more livable. Everyone benefits when people are healthier.

This booklet is one of a series of publications, research, programs, and convocations on the issue of human health and the built environment. Over the next two years, ULI will continue to research and explore health and health-related issues as they relate to the built environment, land use, and the real estate industry. For continuing information on this subject, visit www.uli.org/health.